D1736871

This book is dedicated to everyone who loves to spend time in the bathroom.
Ignore anyone who dares to hammer on the door because they want to use the facilities and get stuck into this book.
Learn fascinating facts about bathrooms, bodily functions, and bounteous trivia!

15 Fast Facts

1. The average person spends about 3 years of their life on the toilet.
2. The first flushing toilet was invented by Sir John Harrington in 1596 for Queen Elizabeth I.
3. In ancient Rome, communal toilets were a common feature, and people used to socialize while using them.
4. The first toilet paper was invented in China in the 6th century, and it was made of rice straw.
5. The first public bathroom in the United States was built in Boston in 1852.
6. The world's oldest working toilet is located in the basement of the Knossos palace on the Greek island of Crete and is over 2,800 years old.
7. The average person uses 57 sheets of toilet paper per day.
8. The first portable toilet was invented in the 1940s for workers on warplanes.
9. The first electric toilet was invented in 1957 by an American inventor named Arnold Cohen.
10. The world's largest public toilet is located in Chongqing, China, and can accommodate over 1,000 people at once.
11. The first bathroom scales were invented in the early 1900s.
12. The average person spends about 1 hour and 45 minutes per week in the bathroom.
13. The world's largest collection of toilets is located in Suweon, South Korea, and features over 4,000 items.
14. The first public restroom for women was installed in New York City's Ladies' Mile shopping district in 1887.
15. The flushing toilet is credited with saving more lives than any other invention in history, as it helped to reduce the spread of infectious diseases.

POOP PUNS

☐	Bake a loaf	☐	Blow Mud
☐	Bomb the bowl	☐	Drop a log
☐	Do the Royal Squat	☐	Dump a Stump
☐	Launch a torpedo	☐	Lay a brick
☐	Make a deposit	☐	Release the payload
☐	Punish the porcelain	☐	Sink the Bismark
☐	Sit on the throne	☐	Offload the brown snake
☐	Plant a tree	☐	Download some software
☐	Pushing brown	☐	Make a delivery
☐	Lay a pipeline	☐	See a man about a dog
☐	Coil one	☐	Evacuate
☐	Grease the bowl	☐	Bake brownies
☐	Lay wolf bait	☐	Deal with an assquake
☐	Touch cloth	☐	Drop the kids at the pool
☐	Cut rope	☐	Birth a food baby

10 Toilet Brush Facts

1) The toilet brush was invented in 1932 by William C. Schopp of Huntington Park, California, US.

2) In 1933, the toilet brush was patented by the Addis Brush Company.

3) The very first toilet brushes were made from wood with pigs' bristles or from the hair of oxen, horses, badgers, or squirrels

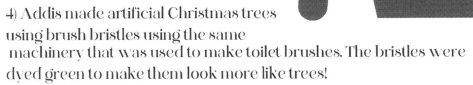

4) Addis made artificial Christmas trees using brush bristles using the same machinery that was used to make toilet brushes. The bristles were dyed green to make them look more like trees!

5) You can buy a designer toilet brush. Philippe Starck has turned a household object into a work of art and it's yours for around $100 .

6) Some people think the best way to clean a toilet brush is to put it into the dishwasher. We don't recommend this!

7) In the UK, a woman had a toilet brush handle stuck in her buttocks for 5 years. She died after an operation to remove it.

8) The latest toilet brushes are made from silicon which is thought to be more hygienic.

9) Toilet brush handles can be made to look like a cactus and the base like a pot giving a whole new look to the bathroom.

10) Toilet brushes should be replaced every 6 months. Try closing the lid on the brush handle and letting it drip dry before you store it to prolong the life of your brush.

Learn British Rhyming Slang

Bees and Honey: Money

Box of Toys: Noise

Cherry Tart: Heart

China: Mate - a shortened version of China plate

Chalk: Arm (Chalk Farm is a place in London)

Duck and Dive: Hide

In and Out: - Snout ie Nose

Satin and Silk: Milk

Frazer-Nash: Slash (pee)

German Bands: Hands

Loop the loop: Soup

Mike and Dave: Microwave

Boat Race: Face

Brown Bread: Dead

Current Bun: Sun

Daisy Roots: Boots

Duke of Kent: Rent

Dustbin Lid: Kid

Jam-Jar: Car

Loaf (of bread): Head

North and South: Mouth

Ones and Twos: Shoes

Pen and Ink: Stink

Pete Tong: Wrong

Plates of Meat: Feet

Porky Pie: Lie

Rabbit (and pork): Talk

Rosy (Rosy Lea): Tea

Ruby Murray: Curry

Scarper (Scapa Flow): Go

Scooby (Doo): Clue

Scotch Eggs: Legs

Skin and Blister: Sister

Syrup (of fig): Wig

Tea Leaf: Thief

Turtle Doves: Gloves

Weasel and Stoat: Coat

Whistle and Flute: Suit of clothes

The USA has won the most Miss Universe contests with 8 titles to its credit. Venezuela has won 7 titles. 5 were claimed by Puerto Rico & the Philippines got 4. In 2015, there was controversy when the Miss Universe host, Steve Harvey, accidentally crowned the wrong person. He crowned Miss Columbia whereas she was, in fact, the first runner-up and Miss Philippines had actually won.
Some stories state that the teleprompter showed the wrong information whilst others claim it was all one big publicity stunt.

The annual Pigasus Award is given to a paranormal fraud and the winner is announced on 1st April by James Randi, a retired magician. The award is sent via telepathy so the receiver will only get the award if they have genuine psychic powers. in 2008, a scientist won who claimed to be able to shoot electromagnetic waves from his eyes.

When the classic animated movie Snow White and the Seven Dwarfs won an honorary Oscar, they received a very special trophy. It consisted of one normal-sized Oscar figurine plus 7 miniature 'dwarf-sized' statuettes. For each Oscar Disney won, he received a miniature Oscar charm. When Walt had 20, he made them into a bracelet for his wife.

On March 12, 2019, a Nubian female goat named Lincoln was elected as the honorary town mayor in Fair Haven, Vermont. She signed the oath of office with her hoof print. She beat more than a dozen candidates, including a gerbil named Crystal and a pacifier-sucking dog named Stella, and celebrated her victory by defecating on the town hall floor.

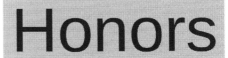

Honors

Loos To Love

Nashville Zoo women's restroom has floor-to-ceiling windows giving an excellent view of the cottontop tamarins monkeys. The men's restroom has a view of the ball python snake exhibit. Let's take a moment to wonder why they chose that particular exhibit...

The J.N. "Ding" Darling National Wildlife Refuge in Sanibel, Florida has 'Learning Lavatories' that include life-size animal sculptures in front of floor-to-ceiling photographs of mangrove scenes. Talk about a 'call of nature'!

Washing your hands at the OdySea Aquarium in Arizona might be a hasty task as 9-foot lemon sharks watch your every move through the wall size windows over the sinks!

If you want to feel like a Princess while doing your business, then head for the Tangled bathrooms in Walt Disney Word Florida. Themed on the story of Rapunzel, elaborate murals decorate the walls and ceiling. The stall doors look like they have come from a stable. Outside, there is often a Disney photographer waiting to record that special moment as you emerge from the restroom. What more could you want!?

Over

- You use less paper because it is easier to see how much you are taking.
- If you use paper with a pattern, then the pattern appears on the top.
- The paper is nearer for someone to reach when required.
- Hotels hang the paper over the roll and often fold it into a neat point at the end although we don't know the point of that!
- Paper that hangs close to the wall could pick up germs from the wall.
- History confirms that the first toilet paper patent diagram had the paper hanging over the roll.
- You don't have to touch other areas in the bathroom to get the paper from the roll.

Under or Over?

Under

- If you hang the paper under the roll, it's slightly harder for cats or toddlers to unravel the whole thing.
- It looks neat and tidy.
- You can make life miserable for other people who may even flip your toilet roll to assume the 'over' position.

However, the worst thing you can do is to leave the empty roll for the next person to replace...

Very Interesting
Body Facts

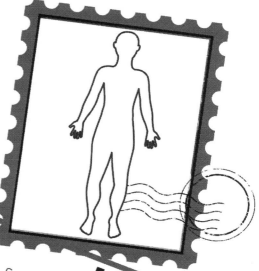

Metabolism

Standing up can burn 50 calories an hour. This is five times more than chewing bubble gum which uses only 10 calories per hour.
Standing for 3 hours a day for 5 days burns 750 calories.
In 2010, a professor lost weight by only eating Twinkies! His calorie intake was lower than the calories burnt so he ultimately lost weight. (He didn't eat many Twinkies even though they were the only thing he ate)

Ears

Scientists have discovered that the left and right ears handle sound a little differently. Your right ear is best for listening to speech. Music, emotion, and intuition are more tuned to your left ear.

Stress

According to a scientific study, traits that tend to make people late are the same traits that can help them live longer and have more productive lives. Science has shown that stress is incredibly bad for overall health and that people who are late typically feel less stressed, unconcerned with deadlines, and generally more relaxed.

Ribs

One out of 200 people has an extra rib. This rib is also medically called a "cervical rib". A cervical rib can be present at birth and it forms above the first rib. You can have a cervical rib on the right, left, or both sides.

Mindblowing Things To Tell Your Friends

Sperm whales vomit up a substance called Ambergris. This waxy substance is found floating in the sea. It has a lovely odor for humans and is the core component of many perfumes

In 1783, a volcanic eruption in Iceland sent so much hydrogen fluoride into the atmosphere that the resulting rain killed 80% of the world's sheep

In 2009, stealth submarines were so effective at hiding themselves, that two of them bumped into each other. Neither submarine could detect the other one, even when they were very close.

In Australia, some birds deliberately increase the spread of wildfires by picking up burning sticks and dropping them elsewhere. The fire forces out their prey making it easier to catch.

When tomatoes were first eaten, so many people died that it was thought that tomatoes were poisonous. However, they were using pewter plates and the acid in the tomatoes reacted with the plates giving people lead poisoning.

The microwave oven inventor only got $2 for his invention. The company he worked for filed the patent and gave him $2 as a bonus

YOUR SENSE OF SMELL IS 10,000 TIMES MORE SENSITIVE THAN YOUR SENSE OF TASTE

Our sense of smell is one of the most important senses we have, and we've evolved our noses to aid our survival in clever ways. The nose is a fantastic warning mechanism, that can alert humans to threats like toxins, smoke, or nasty bathroom pongs.

Your nose is powered by olfactory receptors, which transmit smells as impulses to your brain. This neural pathway goes through your limbic system, the part of your brain strongly associated with emotion. That's why smells can form important parts of our feelings and memories.

We still can't compete with animals like dogs, who can smell anywhere between 10,000 to 100,000 times better than we can.

Scent cells are renewed every 30 to 60 days

You can smell fear and disgust on other people due to the smell of their sweat

Women have a better sense of smell than men

Smell is the oldest sense

Humans each have their own unique odor - just like a fingerprint

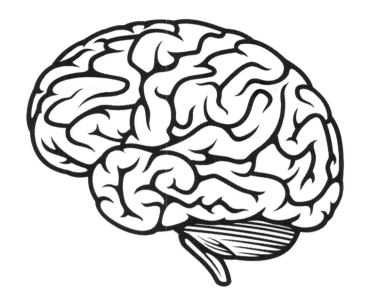

Bizarre Brain fact #1

When you are sleep-deprived, the brain will eat itself.

The process is called phagocytosis, where the brain feeds off of neurons and synaptic connections. The brain is constantly changing its microstructure, and during normal sleep, the glial cells in your brain aim to 'eat' old cells. However, when you stay awake for too long, these cells shift into high gear and start eating healthy brain cells.

HORRIBLE HAUNTINGS

- The Chateau de Brissac castle in France was home to Charlotte who was the illegitimate daughter of King Charles VII. She was murdered by her husband and her ghost haunts the castle. Known as the 'Green Lady' she has been heard moaning in the dead of the night and seen in the chapel's tower room.

- Anne Boleyn, first wife of King Henry VIII, was executed by him at the Tower of London. Now her headless corpse has been seen, on many occasions, wandering the corridors.

- Margaret Pole, Countess of Salisbury had a gruesome execution at the Tower of London. When the executioner raised his axe, the Countess ran away and he chased after her, swinging the axe as he went until finally she died a horrible death. Her ghostly screams echo across Tower Green late at night and some visitors say they have seen a ghostly replay of the chase.

- West Bow house claims to be the most haunted house in Edinburgh, Scotland. Its owner, Major Thomas Weir, was executed in 1670 after he was found guilty of various horrific crimes. His old house then became haunted with visions of unexplained shadows at windows and strange eerie music can be heard coming from the building.

- The Obvodny Canal in St Petersberg, Russia is also known as the 'Suicide Canal'. Those saved from drowning say they don't know what made them jump into the water. Some even say an invisible force pulled them into the water from the bank.

- Buckland Abbey in Devon, England was once owned by Sir Francis Drake. Folklore says that he completed building it because he made a pact with the devil. As a punishment for this, when he died, his ghost was forced to drive a black hearse with four headless horses across nearby moorland.

Bathroom Facts - True or False?

1) There is a day dedicated as 'World Toilet Day'   True False

2) Thomas Crapper invented the toilet   True False

3) The world's most expensive toilet is on the International Space Station   True False

4) There is a toilet museum   True False

5) There are 10 toilets and bathrooms in the White House   True False

6) The more features your smart phone has, the longer you sit on the toilet   True False

7) There are toilet gods   True False

8) The French like red, white, and blue toilet paper to match the tricolor   True False

9) It's OK to flush fish down the toilet bowl   True False

10) You can catch diseases from toilet seats   True False

The text on this page is intentionally upside down to prevent the answers being read accidentally - no spoilers!

Bathroom Facts - True or False?

1) True - Officially sanctioned by the United Nations, World Toilet Day takes place on the 19th November

2) False - He didn't invent the toilet but he did improve the design including the flush

3) True - it cost $19m

4) True - called 'Mr Toilet House', it's located in South Korea

5) False - there are actually 35 to choose from

6) True

7) True - Ancient Romans had a toilet god called Crepitus and he was called upon when an individual was experiencing bouts of diarrhea or constipation

8) False - The French like pink toilet paper whereas the rest of the world prefers white

9) False - Fish flushed away have harmed the ecosystems in which they finally end up

10) False - it's next to impossible to catch a disease from a toilet seat.

9 OF THE MOST DANGEROUS MYTHOLOGICAL MONSTERS

Australian Aborigines talk of a swamp monster called **Bunyip** that hunts children at night. How scary is that?

Scandinavians tell of hairy, cruel **trolls** that live inside the earth and are experts at making things from metal.

The Hound of the Baskervilles is a book that tells the tale of a gigantic, and terrifying, hound from hell.

Greek mythology tells of a **chimera** which was a fire-breathing monster that had the head of a lion and the tail of a snake with the body of a goat.

Medusa was a mythical female monster with many writhing snakes in place of hair. It's said that anyone who looked at her face instantly turned to stone.

Harpies were half female and half bird. They abducted people and tortured them and their name means 'snatchers'.

Typhon was a massive serpent and one of the most deadly creatures in Greek mythology. He had a hundred snake heads and was lawless.

Kappa is part of Japanese folklore and is a type of vampire, greeny-yellow in color with a monkey body but has fish scales instead of hair. Oddly, they can be made docile by giving them a cucumber!

Sirens are legendary ocean creatures with a mermaid form. they are responsible for drownings and shipwrecks as sailors are mesmerised by their beauty and lured onto rocks.

CURIOUS COUNTRIES

The Algerian national anthem entitled "Qassaman" was originally written in blood on a prison wall. It was written by an Algerian revolutionary named Moufdi Zakaria who was incarcerated during the French colonial regime. The music was composed by an Egyptian named Mohamed Fawzi.

In the Netherlands, there's always a teddy bear attached to every Dutch police car, fire truck, and ambulance. The bear helps kids calm down and comforts them at a time of trauma. Some ambulances also use oxygen masks shaped like teddy bears, so that kids will feel more comfortable using the mask.

On the Hawaiian island of Kauai, there's a beach where the sand grains make a sound like a barking dog called, appropriately, the 'Barking Sands Beach'. The dry sand grains have microscopic holes which cause reverberations when touched and rubbed together, especially when someone walks over it with bare feet.

Panama is the only country in the world where you can see the sun rise in the Pacific Ocean and set on the Atlantic Ocean.

In the Yucatan regions of Mexico, living beetles called "makech" are encrusted with jewels and worn as jewelry. They are covered in rhinestones and each beetle has a gold chain and pin that serves as a leash. The bedazzled bug can walk around the wearer's shirt!

WORLD WHAT'S WHAT

The word "gift" in the German language means "poison". In some Scandinavian languages, it means "married". The word "gift" was derived from an Old Norse word "gipt" meaning "give".

In Mexico, artists can pay their taxes using their artworks. The system is called called Pago en Especie (Payment in Kind). This form of tax payment has been used for over six decades and it is still in use today.

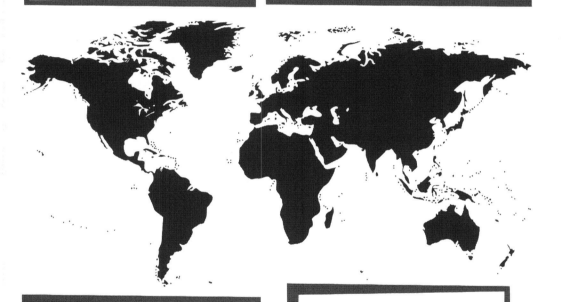

According to a team of Mexican scientists, heated vapor from tequila can form small diamond layers when deposited on a silicon or stainless steel surface. The key to the surprising discovery is tequila's ratio of hydrogen, oxygen, and carbon, which are perfect for growing diamonds.

In 1954, a man jumped off from Golden Gate Bridge in San Francisco because of severe toothache. He was suffering because of a wisdom tooth in the back of his jaw. He had even written a suicide note that simply read: " Absolutely no reason except I have a toothache".

FUN FACTS

In the US, the aptly named Super Bowl halftime show is the moment when more toilets are flushed than any other time in the year

A restaurant in Taiwan serves food in mini toilet bowls - yuk!

The 1960 movie Psycho, was the first to show a toilet flushing. At the time, this was very rude!

Where water is scarce, some toilets burn your waste

Japanese toilets are the most advanced and have heaters, cleaners, and health analysis not to mention music

Flushing the toilet causes bacteria to spray 2m in all directions so keep the lid closed.

WHY DO PEOPLE BUY TOILET ROLL?

When the world is uncertain, people enter a panic mindset. They become irrational and neurotic. Our brains urge us to panic buy even though we have been reassured that there is no need to do this.

We need to take back control in a world where there are factors that affect us that we cannot control.

We enter the supermarket, looking for high volume and value and toilet paper fits the bill nicely. If we see other people also buying toilet paper, we are reassured that this is the correct thing to do. We emerge from the supermarket with a sense of achievement, feeling that we are savvy shoppers – prepared for come what may.

Authority figures can't calm the panic buying. We tend to overemphasize things that are recent and very much in the news e.g. if a plane crash is reported, the number of people flying decreases.

We are seeking control in our lives and wish to make ourselves and our loved ones safe. Our mind then drives us to behave in an unreasonable way – by buying a year's worth of toilet paper.

Our emotions and fears overwhelm the knowledge that we don't need to do this!

INCREDIBLE!!

At the 1908 Olympics, held in London, the Russians showed up 12 days late because they were using the Julian calendar instead of the Gregorian calendar.

In Japan, letting a sumo wrestler make your baby cry is considered good luck and brings the baby good health. The louder the baby cries, the better the luck!

Neil Armstrong's astronaut application arrived a week past the deadline. A friend and colleague secretly added his form to the pile of applicants

The first marketing pitch for the Nerf ball was "Nerf: You can't hurt babies or old people!"

At Petrified Forest National Park, Arizona, visitors sometimes break the law by taking petrified wood home with them. However, shortly after this, the thieves reported being cursed with bad luck. According to rangers, they often end up returning the stolen goods in the mail - along with an apology note.

42% of people pee in the shower

A 10-minute shower uses 180 liters of water.

The biggest shower has a 40ft/12m wide shower head.

The world's longest shower took 340 hours and 40 minutes.

The most people showering in one place at the same time is 145.

The most expensive shower in the world is the $100,000 Silver TAG Shower.
This luxury shower has 18 computer-controlled showerheads, including one that is specially designed for dirty bottoms!
It features six zones which can be individually set for temperature and water pressure.
The whole thing is controlled via a touch screen that is located outside the shower.
If you had the money, would you pay $100,000 for a shower?

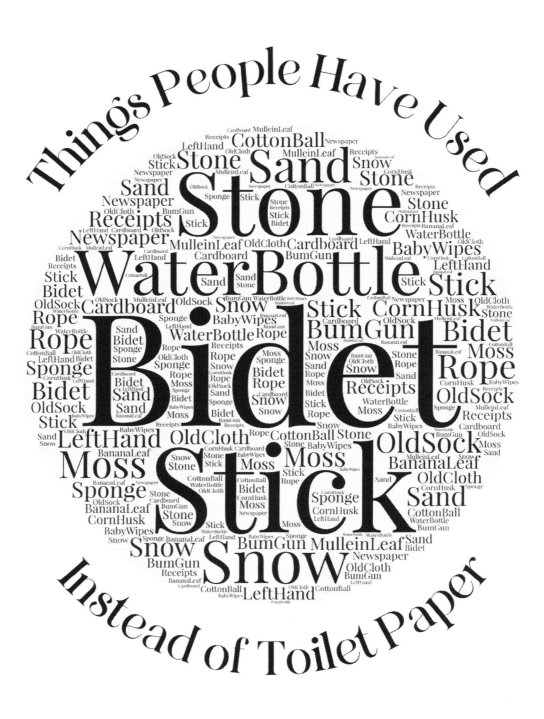

GROSS FACTS ABOUT MEDIEVAL BATHROOMS

WARNING! Do NOT read this whilst eating!
Also, whilst we are on the subject, don't eat in the bathroom
- that's just gross!

CHAMBER POTS were used to collect all the poop and wee overnight. In the morning, the waste was thrown out of the window into the street. Some people had the horrible job of clearing up the muck in the streets - Yuk!

NOSEGAYS, also called Tussie Mussies were small posies of flowers and herbs designed to mask the stench of the street. When you got to a smelly bit, you put the nosegay to your nose and sniffed the beautiful aroma of flowers. Did this actually work?

MOSS and HAY were used in place of toilet paper. A bit scratchy don't you think?

PUBLIC BATHS were the norm in the 13th century. You needed a fire to heat the water and that required wood and took a lot of effort so people used to bathe in public and use water that someone else had used before them!

URINE and ASH from a fire were mixed together and used as a detergent to wash clothes - wonder how they smelt after that?

BATHTIME happened only 4-6 times a year. Water came from a well and had to be heated on the fire. Rumour has it that Queen Elizabeth I only bathed once a year.

HOW WINDY IS THE FART?

Inspired by the Beaufort scale

0
Calm

1
Light puff
Air from the bottom that no one notices

2
Light Breeze
He who smelt it, dealt it

3
Gentle Breeze
Possible trouser ripple

4
Moderate Breeze
Not popular in an elevator

5
Fresh Breeze
Possibly accompanied by a little trump sound

6
Strong Breeze
Forcibly accomplished by the lifting of one cheek

7
High Wind
Embarrassing if you have only just met the person you are with at the time

8
Gale
Arse blast which may impede progress

9
Strong Gale
Eggy and there may be structural damage

10
Storm
Loud thunder and the ground may shake

11
Violent Storm
Vary rarely experienced but similar to a gas attack. Anyone in the vicinity should take cover

12
Hurricane
Devastation
The air is filled with foam and spray and visibility can be affected

Fowl Feces

The Double-Banded Courser bird makes its exrement into an egg shape so that when a predator comes along to snatch an egg to eat, it gets a mouth full of poop instead - YUK!!

The Adele Penguin can shoot its poo quite a distance away from its body in order to keep itself clean. You wouldn't want to be in the firing line!

Nightingale excrement is used in some very expensive anti-wrinkle creams and is supposed to stop skin aging. What are you putting on your face?

The flesh-eating vulture eats dead animals and, as such, ends up with dirty feet. To get its feet clean, it poops on its feet. The poop contains good bacteria that kill off the bad bacteria on their feet. Pretty gross eh?

When designing a skyscraper, architects have to take into account the weight of pigeon poop on the roof.

Some penguin poo is pink! When penguins eat a lot of krill and other crustaceans, it turns their poop pink!!

In the 16th century, pigeon poo was prized as a fantastic fertilizer, and guards were stationed at dovecotes, where the birds were kept, to make sure that the precious poo wasn't stolen!

Bird poop isn't white! Who knew?? The dark part is the poop whereas the white bit is actually uric acid as birds don't make urine and all the waste is excreted as one thing.

Owl pellets are not poop. They are made up of the bones and fur of the previous night's dinner and regurgitated by the owl as a pellet. You can dissect a pellet to see what the owl has eaten!

"Where do you live?"

(embarrassing answers)

USA
Booger Hole, West Virginia

Ding Dong, Texas

Greasy Corner, Arkansas

Hell, Michigan

Intercourse, Pennsylvania

Monkey's Eyebrow, Kentucky

Pee Pee, Ohio

Turkey Scratch, Arkansas

Why, Arizona

UK
Tickle Cock Bridge, West Yorks

Twatt, Shetland

Bottom Flash, Winsford

Bell End, Stourbridge

Willey, Warwickshire

Fan y Big, Brecon

Great Snoring, Fakenham

Shitterton, Bere Regis

Sandy Balls, New Forest

Canada
Punkeydoodles Corners, Ontario

Crotch Lake, Ontario

Blow Me Down, Newfoundland and Labrador

Goobies, Newfoundland and Labrador

Ball's Falls, Ontario

Dude Chilling Park, British Columbia

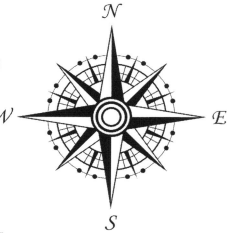

ACQUIRED SAVANT SYNDROME

According to the National Weather Service, you have a 1 in 15,300 chance of getting struck by lightning within your lifetime. Of those unlucky people, 10% would die instantly, whilst 90% would survive with varying degrees of disability.

What statistics don't tell you is that lightning gave someone piano skills.

Tony Cicoria, a New York orthopedist, was struck by lightning in 1994 at 42 years old. Upon recovery, the doctor displayed an uncanny desire to play the piano. He once had taken a couple of lessons as a child but did not enjoy them, yet now he could hear brand-new compositions brewing in his brain and had the urge to write them down.

After learning how to play the piano, he began composing. Even today, he is still playing and his talents and passion for the piano remain.

There are a few similar cases where brain injuries in neurotypical individuals awaken dormant talents. Some experts call this phenomenon Acquired Savant Syndrome, or ASS!

There are at least 50 exceptional ASS cases on record including Alonzo Clemens, a man who developed outstanding sculpting skills following a head injury during a childhood fall.

Another, Orlando Serrell, got hit by a baseball on the left side of his head. He suddenly displayed the ability to perform complex calendrical calculations and can remember every aspect of every day of his life since the accident in 1979.

Experts remain baffled. Could this be proof that all humans have dormant talents within? At this point, it's hard to tell.

If these cases feel oddly similar to superhero backstories, you would be right. However, there is still much to learn about ASS.

DIARRHEA DESIGNATION

- Anal leakage
- Colon Blow
- The squits
- The trots
- The runs
- Whistle belly thumps
- Chocolate thunder
- The Devil's coffee
- Diarizzle
- Hot slurpee
- Fireturds
- Swamp monster
- Pants gravy
- Explodyhole
- Cluster bomb

- Back door trots
- Pebbledash
- Montezuma's revenge
- Havana omelet
- Green apple quick step
- Poop juice
- Poop soup
- The brown flame
- Bubblies
- Trouser chilli
- Nasty Splatty
- Fudge fountain
- Murky waters
- Dire rear
- Super bowels

FAMOUS PLUMBERS

Ozzy Osbourne

A singer-songwriter who once was a skillful plumbing apprentice.

Michael Caine

Actor. Worked as a plumber's assistant whilst pursuing his acting career

Roscoe 'Fatty' Arbuckle

Silent film star who was 'discovered' whilst plumbing for a film producer

John Gotti

John was the head of a crime family and plumbing was their 'front'.

Joe Cocker

Musician. He worked as a plumber whilst establishing his music career

Bob Hoskins

Actor. He was a plumber's assistant in real life and later played a plumber called Mario.

Michael Flatley

Dancer. He had a company called Dynasty Plumbing

Ronnie Lane

Guitarist. Plumbing paid for his first guitar.

Amazing Things To Tell Your Friends

Russia has 6.6 million square miles of land mass whereas Pluto has 6.4 million square miles so Russia is actually bigger than Pluto

Remains of a Pterodactyl were found with a wingspan of 39ft which is bigger than the wingspan of a F16 fighter jet plane

The Burj Khalifa building in Dubai is so tall (2,722 ft, 829.8m) that you can enjoy two sunsets every day. Watch the first from the base of the building then take the elevator to the top to watch the sunset again.

The British Queen used her handbag to give out silent instructions to her staff. If she moved the bag from one arm to the other, she wanted to end a conversation and staff would intervene to move her on.

The South Pacific Ocean has Point Nemo which is the furthest place on the Earth from land. It's used as a scrapyard for spacecraft and contains over 300 items including spacecraft and space debris

High-heeled shoes were originally worn by men. The Persian cavalry wore them as the heels helped to keep their boots in stirrups when they were riding.

Digestion Details

Stomach rumbling is called 'Borborygmi

Your stomach can stretch to hold up to 4lb (2kg) of food

If you stretched out your small intestine, it would cover a tennis court

Most food is digested in the small intestine not the stomach

The stomach produces 4 pints (2 liters) of hydrochloric acid per day

Your food is broken down by enzymes and some laundry detergents use the same enzymes

The first time a doctor looked inside someone's stomach, they had to use a sword swallower as the camera tube was rigid

If you vomit, extra saliva is produced to protect your teeth from the acid

Every day, your body makes 2 pints (1 liter) of saliva

Your digestive system does not need gravity to work. Your muscles push the food along

Learn British Slang

Drunk:
Trollied / Plastered/ Hammered / Legless/ Half-Cut /
Drunk as a skunk / Tanked up / Bevvied / Paralytic /
Rat arsed / Merry / Under the influence / Off their face /
Three sheets to the wind / Pissed as a fart / Well oiled /
Drunk as a Lord / In her cups / Blotto / Wellied / Sloshed /
Squiffy / Out of their tree / Can't lie down without holding on

Money:
Quid / Dosh/ Readies / Smakeroonies / Filthy Lucre / Brass /
Wonga / Bread / Dough / Fiver / Loot / Tenner / Grand

Tired:
Knackered / Cream crackered / Frazzled / Clapped Out /
Shattered / Bushed / Pooped / Fried

Terms of Endearment:
Poppet / Sweetheart / Hen / Maid / Babes / Treacle /
Sweetie / Hun / Cutie / Pet / Bubba / Cherub / Hubby

Nonsense:
Codswallop / Poppycock / Bunkum / Claptrap / Tripe /
Mumbo Jumbo / Tommyrot /Load of Old Cobblers / Drivel /
Piffle / Twaddle / Waffle / Flannel

Goodbye:
Toodle-Pip / Ta-Ta / Pip-Pip / Laters / Cheerio

PROJECT ACOUSTIC KITTY

When it comes to tinfoil conspiracies, few institutions are as omnipresent as the Central Intelligence Agency, and it's not hard to see why when they're known for a sizeable number of ridiculously-sounding projects.

Cue Acoustic Kitty, a project declassified in 2001 that seems straight out of an Adam Sandler movie script.

During the 60s and amidst the Cold War, the CIA's main goal was to undermine Soviet efforts in every conceivable way. Under that perception, they sought ways to fulfil the American duty of spying on Soviet embassies.

But at some point, a genius had a revolutionary idea—What if we used cats?

Thus, Project Acoustic Kitty was born—an honest effort by the American government to turn cats into trained spies. Proof that no one in the CIA headquarters had ever owned a cat.

The plan was to install equipment on the cats to capture and transmit sounds. The CIA thought cats' stealthy ways and curious nature would make them perfect for the task, yet they forgot to account for one notorious cat trait: they don't care.

It is here that the story turns from funny to outright terrifying. The cats were cut open and had batteries and other devices installed inside. Project Acoustic Kitty took five years to develop, and although it isn't mentioned, it's safe to assume many cats died in the process.

It was all for nothing. After successfully preparing a cat, they released it for its first mission. It proceeded to do what cats do—go its own way against instructions. Sadly, the poor cat got killed by a taxi.

It was only then that the CIA realized that maybe this was a bad idea. Sadly, it took them several animal deaths and $20 million in investment to reach this conclusion.

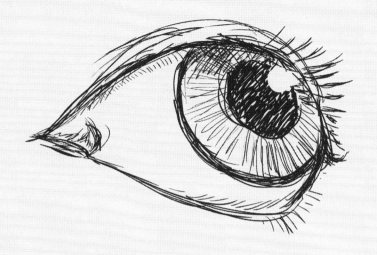

RANDOM FACT

The human
eye blinks an
average of
4,200,000
times a year.

SCIENCE STORIES

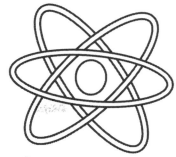

- The howling winds that blow 3,000 miles from the Sahara desert, and cross the Atlantic Ocean, carry dusts that are rich in phosphorus. These phosphorus-enriched dusts act as natural fertilizers for the soils of Amazon rainforests.

- Brass doorknobs automatically disinfect themselves every 8-12 hours. They have a property called "oligodynamic effect" which is toxic to living cells, molds, algae, spores, fungi, viruses, prokaryotic and eukaryotic microorganisms.

- In 2013, scientists found trace amounts of gold on the leaves of eucalyptus trees in Australia. The particles are much too small to be seen with the naked eye but can be detected by using a type of X-ray that can detect trace amounts of minerals and metals.

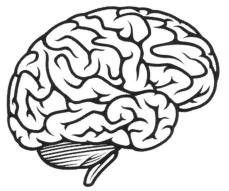

- Sleep actually cleans your brain. During the night, cerebrospinal fluid flushes through the brain and washes away harmful proteins and toxins that build up during the day.

History

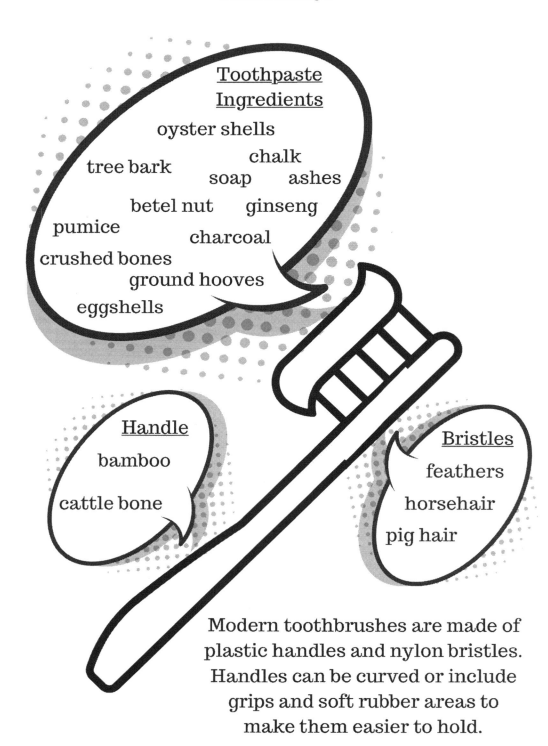

Toothpaste Ingredients
oyster shells
chalk
tree bark
soap   ashes
betel nut   ginseng
pumice
charcoal
crushed bones
ground hooves
eggshells

Handle
bamboo
cattle bone

Bristles
feathers
horsehair
pig hair

Modern toothbrushes are made of plastic handles and nylon bristles. Handles can be curved or include grips and soft rubber areas to make them easier to hold.

To Boldly Go

Astronaut urine is filtered and processed and the astronauts drink it again as water and again and again...

Space toilets have a special funnel for urine and a little seat for poo. Both can be used at the same time.

The space loo has places to hold your feet and grab points so that astronauts don't float away whilst in position.

Toilet tissue and wipes are put into water-tight bags. The bags are placed with poo bags into a cannister which are then loaded into a cargo ship that burns up upon re-entry as it passes through the Earth's atmosphere.

The space toilet is situated inside a stall just like in a normal restroom.

There are 2 toilets on the International Space Station.

The latest NASA space toilet cost $23m to develop and can be used by women as well as men. Some of it is made with 3D printing and it uses metals that do not erode when subjected to uric acid.

WORLD TOILET DAY

WORLD TOILET DAY takes place on November 19 each year and was created by the United Nations to highlight the fact that 4.2 billion people around the world do not have 'safely managed sanitation'.

<u>THEMES</u>

2012 - I give a shit, do you?

2013 - Tourism and water

2014 - Equality and Dignity

2015 - Toilets and Nutrition

2016 - Toilets and Jobs

2017 - Wastewater

2018 - When Nature Calls

2019 - Leaving no one behind

2020 - Sustainable sanitation and climate change

40% of the people do NOT have basic hand washing facilities at home

Globally, 80% of waste water goes back into the ecosystem without being treated or reused

By 2050, up to 5.7 billion people will be living in an area where water is scarce for at least one month of the year

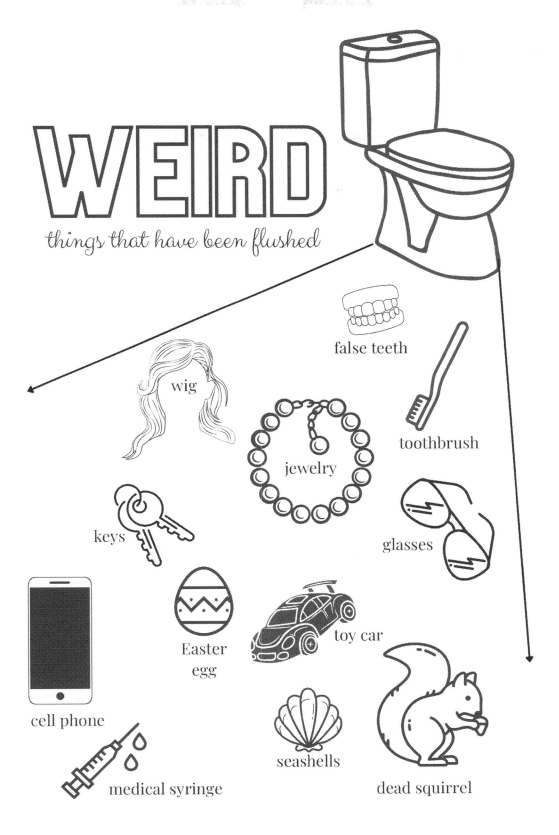

Never Ask The General Public

(when voting contests go wrong)

The UK held a voting contest to name a research ship and the overall winning name was 'Boaty McBoatface'. This sparked copycat names with an Australian ferry boat being named 'Ferry McFerryface' and a pipe inspecting robot in Kansas City having the suggested name of 'Probey McProbeface'.

Greenpeace made the mistake of asking the public to name an endangered humpback whale and took it to a public vote. The winning name was 'Mister Splashy Pants'.

A ferry company regretted asking the public to name one of its ferries and the entries included 'SS ShouldveBeenABridge', 'Queen of No Other Choice', and 'Spirit of the WalletSucker'.

A council in the UK asked for names for its road gritters which spread salt on the roads in icy conditions.
Popular choices included:
Gritsy Bitsy Teeny Weeny Yellow Anti-Slip Machinery
David Plowie
Grit Balls o'Fire
Spready Mercury
Basil Salty
Grit Van Dyke
Gritney Spears
The Subzero Hero
Mr Plow
Usain Salt
Walter the Salter
Rule Gritannia
Gritney Houston

Gritsy Bitsy Teeny Weeny Yellow Anti-Slip Machiney won the public vote and was adopted by the council.

PERPLEXING PLACES

- Stonehenge is a circle of standing stones each up to 30ft (9m) tall. The circle was placed around 4000-5000 years ago. The stones are arranged such that on the 21st of June each year, the Summer Solstice, the sun shines into the entrance of the circle. There are many theories but no one knows why Stonehenge exists or how it was built.

- The Nazca plains in Peru are etched with lines, mostly created with shallow trenches. Some lines form the shapes of animals including a pelican, a lizard, and a monkey. Experts cannot agree on why the lines are there and there are many different theories.

- Over 200 planes and ships have vanished in an area of the ocean called the Bermuda Triangle. Some think that there are strange magnetic forces here that make compasses inaccurate and others think the weather is to blame. No one knows for sure.

- In the US, Shale Creek in Western New York houses a very strange waterfall. Behind the water, there is an eternal flame tht scientists think is fueled by natural gas escaping from the rock but they can't be certain.

- The Sahara desert is home to a perfect set of circular concentric rings that can only be seen from the air. Scientists think it could be caused by the impact of an asteroid but other people think it is a naturally occurring geological feature. A wackier idea is that aliens made the circles...

- The crooked forest in Poland has trees that bend over by 90 degrees before curving upright. Surrounding trees are straight and no one knows why some of the trees are mysteriously curved in this way.

Stinking Rich?

A UNIVERSITY IN SOUTH KOREA HAS A TOILET THAT TURNS POOP INTO MONEY FOR THE STUDENTS WHO USE IT.

THE TOILET IS CONNECTED TO A FACILITY THAT USES THE POOP TO GENERATE BIOGAS.

THE POOP IS PUMPED TO A TANK AND WASTE WATER IS REMOVED.

MICROORGANISMS BREAK DOWN THE POOP INTO METHANE.

THE METHANE IS USED FOR ENERGY IN THE BUILDING INCLUDING BOILING WATER.

THE AVERAGE PERSON PRODUCES ENOUGH POOP EACH DAY TO MAKE 50 LITERS OF METHANE GAS.

STUDENTS WHO USE THE TOILET GET PAID IN A VIRTUAL CURRENCY CALLED GGOOL.

EACH TOILET USE GETS THEM 10 GGOOL.

THEY CAN USE THE GGOOL TO BUY COFFEE, NOODLES, FRUIT OR BOOKS.

Loos To Love

The Saskatchewan Science Center lets you do your business surrounded by the sights and sounds of nature without worrying that the bears might get you!

The walls have floor-to-ceiling images of the Canadian forest and birdsong plays while you get comfortable.

The idea is to create an 'outhouse in the woods experience'!

A restaurant in London has toilet cubicles shaped like white eggs. Once inside, the visitor hears eerie music and sees color-changing LED lights.

Some First Class airplane toilets have windows! It's possible to enjoy a loo-view of the Pyramids shortly before landing in Cairo. Selfie, anyone?

Very Interesting

Animal Facts

Ostrich

The ostrich egg is the world's largest egg of any living bird. It weighs over 20 times the weight of the chicken egg. It takes about 50 minutes to be soft-boiled and 90 minutes to get hard-boiled.

Newt

The Iberian ribbed newt uses its own ribs as weapons by voluntarily protruding its rib cage along its spine. When the sharp ends poke out through the skin, it excretes venom and stings its predator.

Ants

Ants have 4-5 times more odor receptors than most other insects. They have special proteins in their receptors that detect odors. Ants can distinguish about 400 different odors

Angry Zebra

If a zebra gets bad-tempered, it can't release its bite. When seriously enraged, their kicks are powerful enough to kill a person. This is one of the main reasons why zebras cause more injuries to US zookeepers than any other animals.

Crabs

Some crabs, including a species called Ghost Crabs, have teeth in their stomach. They use their teeth to process food and also to growl at one another during aggressive interactions. Grrrrrrrrrrr

Extreme Excrement

Parrot fish eat coral using a beak which is shaped like a parrot's. Their excrement is pure sand as they convert the coral to sand as it passes through their body!

Some spiders disguise themselves as bird excrement so that they don't get eaten.. The orb spider has a silver web and a silver body and birds think it is poop!

When a hippo poops, it spins its tail around like a fan to scatter its excrement wide and far. This is to mark their territory and to impress females.

Pandas poop up to 50 lbs/22 kg of excrement per day!

Monkeys just love to throw around their excrement! Firstly, it was a way to defend themselves then it became a bit of fun – Don't try this at home!

AMAZING!!

Flyting is the exchange of witty, insulting verses. They were popular in England and Scotland from the 5th - 16th centuries.

In 1962, the Volvo car company gave away the patent for their revolutionary three-point seat belt for free to save as many lives as possible.

Melbourne, Australia allocated email addresses to some of its trees so that people could report problems. Instead, they received love letters and existential queries.

In the US, an estimated 1 million dogs have been named as the main beneficiary in their owners' wills.

The lamp posts in Central Park, New York each display four numbers to help you navigate. The first two numbers indicate the nearest street, and the next two tell you whether you're closer to the East or West side of the park (even numbers indicate East, odd numbers, West).

Outer Space

In outer space, there's a cloud made from alcohol. It is about 1000 times the diameter of our entire solar system. There is enough alcohol to supply every person on Earth with 300,000 pints of beer every day for the next billion years.

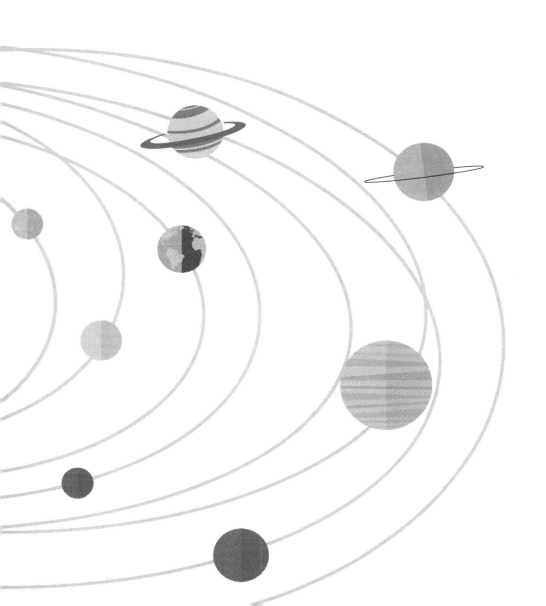

THE WORLD'S WORST VIDEOGAME

If you are an avid gamer, odds are you have strong opinions regarding the 'worst game ever made'. An objective analysis of pop-culture history reveals the dishonorable title arguably belongs to Atari's E.T. The Extraterrestrial.

After the success of Raiders of the Lost Ark, the thriving videogame company Atari got the rights to turn it into a videogame, and Howard Warshaw had the duty to bring it to life.

Back then storytelling didn't matter much for games, but Warshaw wanted his to match the movie. It took him ten months to put it together, but even Steven Spielberg himself recognized the talent and loved the results.

Thus, when it was time to make a video game about Spielberg's next hit, E.T. The Extra-Terrestrial, Warshaw was the man for it.

But there was a problem. Atari and Spielberg's lengthy negotiations extended until July 1982. The company wanted to sell the game during the Christmas season, and that meant Warshaw only had a short time until September to finish making the game.

He had a tight deadline of only five weeks. But thought he could handle it.

Instead of going for a simpler route, he wanted the game to be as complex as his previous ones. The result was a chaotic, senseless, and impossible game that no one liked and sales plummeted.

The market was saturated with equally low-quality games by that time, which led to an inevitable collapse in the market. Atari couldn't handle the crisis, and it soon vanished from the game industry.

Soon after the crash, an urban legend developed that the company had buried millions of unsold copies in the New Mexico desert. It became a widespread conspiracy theory and an excavation in 2014 confirmed it.

Distracting Details

Leonardo da Vinci

Aside from being an artist and an inventor, Leonardo da Vinci was also a famous wedding planner! He is also is credited with the invention of scissors. Some historians also think he invented the napkin. Leonardo had a strong interest in dining etiquette. Who knew?!!

Lego

The world's largest LEGO tower was built in Milan, Italy on June 21, 2015. It was 114ft and 11" (35.05m) tall and used a total of 550,000 bricks. It was visited by 50,000 spectators and it took 18,000 people to build the tower. To stop it from falling over, metal cables were attached to the tower and anchored to the ground.

Super Mario

The mushrooms used in the Super Mario video game were based on a fungus, Amanita Muscaria. It has a hallucinogenic effect which makes users feel as though they are growing gradually bigger.

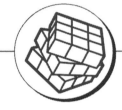

Rubik's Cube

In 1974, it took one month for the Rubik creator, Erno Rubik, to solve his own Rubik's cube puzzle. Now, the world's fastest speedcuber is Yusheng Du. He was 22 years old and solved the puzzle in just 3.47 seconds. A robot has even solved the puzzle in just 0.38 seconds! How long would it take you??

Strong earthquakes can make the Earth spin faster and can even shorten the day in a minimal amount of time. One example is during the 2011 Japanese earthquake. According to a geophysicist from NASA named Richard Gross, this earthquake has decreased the length of the day by 1.8 microseconds.

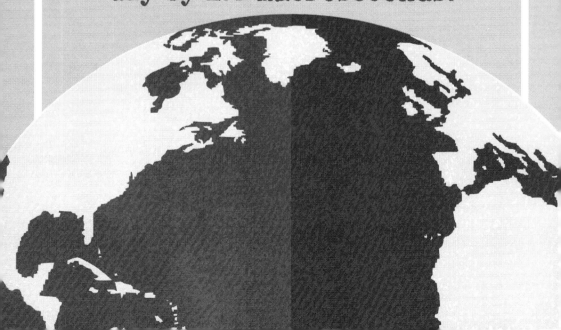

WORLD WHAT'S WHAT

Genghis Khan, a former Mongol emperor, was responsible for the death of approx.. 40 million people during his reign between 1172 and 1127.

New York is considered to be the most linguistically diverse, multicultural city in the world. There are more than 800 languages spoken on a daily basis in the city. It has also the largest population of immigrants on the entire planet with over 35% of residents born outside the US.

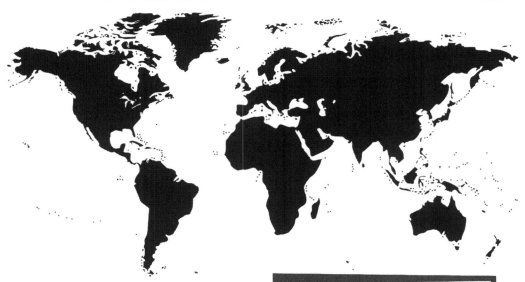

The construction of one of the world's most famous pieces of Greek architecture, the Parthenon, involved almost no straight lines or right angles. It has withstood earthquakes, fire, wars, explosions and even looting. It is estimated that 13,400 stones were used to build the temple.

According to a 2000 Japanese poll, Japan's best invention, as voted by its citizens, was instant noodles. Karaoke came in second place. Third place went to headphone stereo sets. In seventh place is the great filmmaker Akira Kurosawa who is not technically an invention!

How to Write English Good:

- It is wrong to ever split an infinitive.

- Contractions aren't necessary

- The passive voice is to be avoided.

- Prepositions are not the right words to end sentences with.

- Try to be more or less specific.

- Go all around the houses to avoid colloquialisms.

- One-word sentences? Eliminate.

- Who needs rhetorical questions?

- Exaggeration is a billion times worse than understatement.

- You should of used 'should have'.

FASCINATING FOLK

Adam Rainer of Austria is the only person in recorded medical history who has been classified as both a dwarf and a giant in his lifetime. He had a dwarfism characteristic with an adult height of below 147 cm (4 ft. 0.25 in). When he reached the age of 33, he had a dramatic growth spurt due to a pituitary tumor and reached a height of 218 cm (7 ft. 2 in.). He is believed to have had acromegaly — an abnormal growth of the hands, feet, and face caused by the overproduction of growth hormone by the pituitary gland.

In 1991, a couple from Sweden named their son Brfxxccxxmnpcccclllmmnprxvcl mnckssqlbb11116 which is pronounced as "Albin". The parents give their child this name as a protest against a fine which is imposed in accordance with the naming law in Sweden. Because the parents had failed to register a name by the boy's fifth birthday, a district court in Halmstad, southern Sweden, fined them 5,000 kronor (roughly $740 at the time).

Amelia Earhart and Eleanor Roosevelt once sneaked out of a White House dinner, commandeered an airplane, and went on a joyride to Baltimore and back to Washington.
After the flight was over, they returned to the White House and finished the meal with dessert.

Incredible Things To Tell Your Friends

In the 1990s, you had to put a CD into your computer to sign up to use an internet service. At this time, half of the world's CDs were AOL sign-up CDs

In 1997, a container ship was hit by a large wave and some of the cargo was washed overboard including 4.8 million pieces of Lego. They are still being found on UK beaches today.

You can cuddle a hedgehog whilst enjoying a hot chocolate at a cafe in Tokyo, Japan.

At the Wimbledon tennis tournament, balls are kept at 68 degrees Fahrenheit (20 degrees Celcius). The balls are filled with air and the temperature affects the bounce quality.

The Belgians thought it would be a great idea to use cats to deliver letters. They put the letters into waterproof bags and tied them around the cats' necks. However, the cats proved slow and unreliable so the idea was dropped.

The pose of a horse in a statue tells you how the rider died. If both front legs are in the air, the rider died in battle. If one leg is in the air, the rider died of wounds sustained in battle and if both front legs are on the ground, the rider died of natural causes

DID YOU KNOW?

The bones in your forearm cross when you twist your arm

Most people consider bones to be straight and rigid, but did you know the bones in your forearm cross when you twist them? The two bones in your forearm are known as the ulna and the radius.

When your arm is outstretched, they run parallel to each other, but as soon as you turn, they cross over. It's super freaky!

DID YOU KNOW?

We share 70% of our DNA with a slug

Next time you see a slug, you could be talking to a cousin! Well, that is a cousin of the human race. We humans share around 70% of our DNA with slugs. We also share 50% of our DNA with bananas.

Other cool DNA similarities include a 44% match with honey bees, 50% with trees, and even 25% with daffodils. If humans started a dating app for DNA matches, you could match with a daffodil!

BATHROOM BRANDING

- Thunderbox
- Throne room
- Oval office
- Thinking throne
- Wizzer
- Glory hole
- The penthouse
- Situation room
- Powder room
- Privy
- House of office
- Garderrobe
- Biffy
- Poo snuggler
- Kerplunk

- Stool pool
- Wiz box
- Khazi
- Snakehouse
- Underwater log cabin
- Stink lodge
- Urination station
- One man floor plan
- Poopalorium
- Bogger
- Netty
- Honey bucket
- Little boys room
- Pooptrap
- Kybo (keep your bowels open)

Pay As You Go?

SOMETIMES YOU HAVE TO PAY TO USE THE TOILET. THE MONEY IS USUALLY USED TO CLEAN AND MAINTAIN THE EQUIPMENT.

IN THE USA, PAY TOILETS BECAME LESS COMMON IN THE 1970S BECAUSE WOMEN OBJECTED TO PAYING FOR A TOILET STALL WHEN MEN USED URINALS FREE OF CHARGE.

IN THE UK, PAY TOILETS TEND TO BE COMMON AT BUS AND RAILWAY STATIONS BUT MOST PUBLIC TOILETS ARE FREE OF CHARGE.
THE EXPRESSION 'SPEND A PENNY' COMES FROM USING A PRE-DECIMAL PENNY IN TOILET LOCKS.

IN INDIA, TOILETS HAVE AN ATTENDANT AND COST 2 RUPEES. THEY SOMETIMES HAVE BATHROOM FACILITIES FOR WASHING AS WELL AS TOILETS FOR AREAS WITH POOR SANITATION.

IN MEXICO, PUBLIC TOILETS HAVE TURNSTILES AND AN ATTENDANT AT THE ENTRANCE. THE ATTENDANT HANDS THE USER A DESIGNATED AMOUNT OF TOILET PAPER WHEN THE FEE IS PAID.

IN PLACES WHERE THERE IS POOR SANITATION, LANDLORDS CAN USE THE EXISTENCE OF PAY TOILETS AS A REASON NOT TO INSTALL A PRIVATE TOILET FOR THEIR TENANTS.

IT CAN BE ARGUED THAT CHARGING TO USE A PUBLIC TOILET IS IMMORAL AS THIS IS A BASIC HUMAN RIGHT.

PAID TOILETS ADVERSELY AFFECT THE ELDERLY, DISABLED, PREGNANT WOMEN, CHILDREN, AND THE HOMELESS.

Wonderful Woofs

Dogs are capable of understanding up to 250 words and gestures. The average dog is as intelligent as a two-year-old child.

Dogs can detect sadness in humans. They will often initiate cuddling just to make them feel happier. A study published in the journal " Animal Cognition" found that a dog was more likely to give attention to someone who was upset and crying rather than someone who was doing something generic like talking or humming.

Dogs can be trained to sniff out medical issues. They can detect low blood sugars, and oncoming epileptic attacks and some are even being trained to detect Covid-19!

Dogs can sniff at the same time as breathing!

Some dogs are fantastic swimmers. The Newfoundland breed of dog is even trained to rescue people from water.

Greyhound dogs can run very fast and have the stamina to keep this up for several miles.

Dogs can't sweat so they pant to cool down.

Dogs have a dominant paw just as humans have a dominant hand.

Dogs have 18 muscles that control their ears. That's why dogs move their ears around so much!

AMAZING ANIMALS

Iguanas have a third eye called the parietal eye. This eye looks like a normal body scale but is paler. It senses light and movement and helps them see predatory birds flying up above their heads.

Rabbits and hares eat their night poop to get extra nutrition. This activity is called coprophogia and their night stools are called cecotropes. This disgusting 'food' contains enough protein & vitamins to stop malnutrition.

Baby hippos enjoy licking and gently biting crocodiles. The crocs tolerate this and do not attack them. Scientists think this might be because the crocs are frightened of hippo parents but no one really knows.

The animal on Earth with the most legs is a white millipede and it is found in California. It has a staggering 750 legs! A scientist found the millipede in 2005 but before that, it had not been seen for nearly 80yrs.

The eyes of Arctic reindeer change color depending on the time of year. Summer:gold and Winter:blue. The clever color change allows them to adapt to the changing light levels in their extreme habitat where Summers have 24 hours of daylight and Winters have none..

Cats and dogs make happy hormones called oxytocin and dogs produce 5 times the amount of oxytocin than cats. This makes them more social and interactive with humans. Cats take a much longer time to form inseparable bonds with their owners.

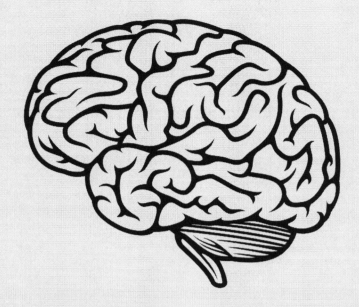

Bizarre Brain fact #2

When you blink, parts of your brain are turned off.

This amazing fact solves one of life's biggest mysteries.

A team from UCL found in 2005 that, when you blink, your brain shuts down parts of your visual cortex to give you an "uninterrupted view of the world". This finding could explain why we don't notice our blinks.

The scientists at the Institute of Neurology say our brain does this so we don't go into panic when the world goes dark.

FASCINATING!!

Bloodcurdling isn't just an expression: Research shows that watching horror movies can increase a certain clotting protein in our bloodstream.

The Mobile Phone Throwing World Championships are held in Finland. Competitors can pick from an array of phones provided by the sponsor
The world record is 362.3ft (110.42m)

Elvis Presley's manager sold badges saying 'I Hate Elvis' and 'Elvis is a Jerk' so that he could make money off of people who weren't buying his fan merch.

In April 1930, the BBC announced that 'There is no news' and instead of reading the news, they broadcast piano music for 15 minutes.

LEGO has a not-so-secret underground vault in Billund, Denmark. It contains every set they've ever made from the 1950s to the present day. The vault is secure, temperature and humidity-controlled and fireproof.

Learn British Phrases

Lost the plot: No idea what is happening

Bee's Knees: The best thing or person ever

Know your onions: Knowledgeable about a particular subject

Dog's Bollocks: awesome

Bob's your uncle: There you go ie something is completed

Throw a spanner in the works: Something has gone wrong

Dog's Dinner: A mess

Don't get your knickers in a twist: Stay calm

Bits 'n' Bobs: various small items

Up the wooden hill to Bedfordshire: Going to bed

Meat and two veg: Men's genitalia

Brass monkeys outside: Very cold outside

Chip off the old block: A kid who is similar to their parent

Chocolate teapot: An item which is useless

Chuffed as nuts: Very pleased

Climbing the walls: Impatiently waiting for something

Jammy Dodger: Someone who is lucky

Tickety-boo: Something going well

Cooking with gas: Something going well

Mad as a box of frogs: a crazy situation or person

The penny has dropped: Someone finally understands

Put wood in the hole: Shut the door

What's the damage?: How much does it cost?

Remarkable Things

No one knows who invented the first fire hydrant because the patent was destroyed. No one is exactly sure how this happened but popular theories include fires, floods, and even a heated argument caused that the eradication of the patent.

The world's oldest light bulb has been shining since 1901. It is called the Centennial Light and is found at 4550 East Avenue, Livermore, California. It is maintained by the Livermore-Pleasanton Fire Department. Former American president George Bush has even sent letters to acknowledge its longevity.

You can buy a huge firework called the Super Crown. It is 2 ft (0.6m) and holds 75lb (34 kg) of gunpowder and explosives. The first charge fires it 1,600ft (488 m) into the air then a second charge scatters golden stars across approximately a quarter of a mile.

Before the firework can be sent skywards, the user has to dig a hole 6ft (2m) deep from which the firework can be launched.

Humans & elephants are the only animals to have chins

Believe it or not, no other species barring us and our elephant cousins have chins. Even our closest living relatives the chimpanzees and gorillas don't have chins. Their lower jaws slope down instead of forwards.

The weirdest thing about our weird chins is that scientists can't agree on why we're the only ones to have them. Not even Neanderthals had them. Do we know why elephants have them? Absolutely not.

They're so unique to us that archaeologists use chins to distinguish whether or not skeletons are homo-sapiens (humans) or not.

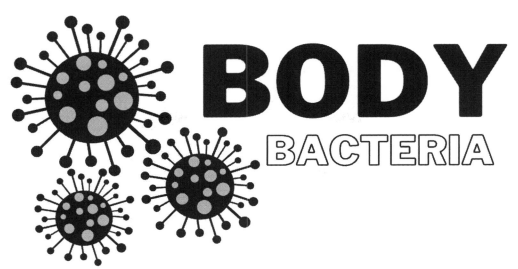

BODY BACTERIA

HUMANS CARRY AROUND FOUR POUNDS (1.8KG) OF BACTERIA IN THEIR BODIES.

That's enough to fill around a soup can of microbes. Most of these bacteria live in our gut and helps us with digestion. In fact, having bacteria in our bodies helps keep us healthy.

We humans rely on bacteria so much that there is ten times the number of bacteria cells in our body than our own human cells. Technically, people are just vessels for bacteria. Gross.

MORE GERMS ARE TRANSFERRED BY SHAKING HANDS THAN BY KISSING.

Our hands are gross. Scientists have found that handshakes transfer around 124 million bacteria to our unsuspecting hosts. This is compared to only around 80 million bacteria making the jump during a ten-second intimate kiss.

However, there is one form of contact that trumps both of these: keyboards and computer mice. The average desktop keyboard possesses up to 400 times more bacteria than the average toilet seat. Yuck. The moral of this story has to be to always sanitize your keyboard.

THE TITANIC & THE TITAN

The world is filled with coincidences so unlikely and fascinating that the human brain refuses to believe they lack meaning.

One such captivating event is on the pages of The Wreck of the Titan: Or, Futility, a novella published in 1898 by Morgan Robertson. It was not a literary masterpiece, and it would have been forgotten entirely if a tragedy had not taken place on April 15, 1912.

Audiences quickly noticed the tale of the Futility showed eerie parallels with the sinking of the RMS Titanic - 14 years before it took place.

The ship featured in Futility was named Titan, a British construction considered the largest and built to be perfect and unsinkable, with a capacity for over 3,000 people. Just like the Titanic.

But those are only the surface-level coincidences.

Robertson described the Titan in excruciating detail, and its structure was nearly identical to the Titanic's—same size, speed, number of propellers, masts, and even the same deficient number of lifeboats.

Although unnerving, the coincidences jump from strange to baffling when it comes to the fate of both ships.

Both the fictitious Titan and the actual Titanic hit an iceberg in the North Atlantic Ocean on an April night close to midnight. The point of impact in both cases was starboard. The Titan's speed of impact was 25 knots, and the Titanic's was 22.5.

Despite the near-supernatural coincidence, Robertson scoffed at being called a clairvoyant. He was the son of a ship's captain and an experienced seaman and could predict the disaster simply because he knew all about the subject.

Understanding the sea, he knew that icebergs were a risk in the Atlantic and he understood trends in ship design. But how can expertise explain the eerily similar names, dates of impact, or location?

There is only one letter of the alphabet that does not appear in any US State name. It is Q. You might have guessed Z but that's in Arizona or J (New Jersey) or X (Texas).

Scotland has 421 different words to describe snow including Spitters (small drops of snow), Skelf (a large snowflake), and Feefle (swirling snow)

Armadillos have shells that are bulletproof. One man in Texas was hit by a bullet that ricocheted off an armadillo and hit him in the face.

Firefighters make water wetter by adding agents to reduce the surface tension so that the water spreads more easily and soaks into objects.

Human noses and ears continue to grow slowly throughout your life

The word 'fizzle' originally meant to break wind quietly.

Kleenex tissues were originally invented as a filter for gas masks.

Blue whales eat half a million calories in each mouthful of krill.

There's a tiny pocket in your jeans and it's designed to store a pocket watch.

NASA can get new items to astronauts by email. They are actually instructions for a 3D printer so that the astronauts can print new tools in just a few hours.

Most of the Sahara desert is covered in gravel, not sand.

Humans are the only animals that can cry

Did you know that we are the only animals that have the ability to produce emotional tears? Animals can create tears but they use them solely to lubricate their eyes. This doesn't mean that animals can't feel emotions like sadness and grief, as any pet owner will know well. But, in the animal kingdom, outward displays of emotions like crying are much rarer.

In fact, naturalists like Charles Darwin argued that crying serves no adaptive function and that by crying we humans have gained no evolutionary advantage. It does however feel good to cry, so we should do what we wish.

The reasons why we cry also change with age. Powerlessness and being apart from people we love will make us cry throughout our lives.
Children cry as a result of physical pain but this is less common in adults. Adults are more likely to cry for sentimental reasons e.g. if they see someone doing good things for others.
Adults are also more likely to cry about the distress and suffering of other people.

10 THINGS THAT MAKE HUMANS SPECIAL

1. We can speak thanks to a larynx

2. Our brains are extraordinary

3. We wear clothes for protection and fashion

4. We are the only primate that walks upright

5. We can extend our thumb across the palm

6. We have much longer childhoods than other primates

7. We are naked compared to apes who have fur

8. We can control fire and use it for cooking

9. We blush although no one knows why

10. Females survive even though they can no longer reproduce

WEIRD

things that have been flushed

Animals

It's well known that goldfish have been flushed down the toilet but what about other animals?

Animals that have been discovered in toilets, both flushed and unflushed, and include: puppies, opossums, snakes, an iguana, a shark, and large fish.

Sometimes, kids are trying to wash a pet animal and it falls in but some animals just get into the toilet all by themselves.

People

It's hard to believe, but people have been found in toilets!

In one case, a man hid in a septic tank so that he could look up at women using the toilet – some people are really weird and freaky.

Money

A toilet cleaner in Australia once found $93,000 whilst cleaning a toilet. The police could not find the owner so the finder was allowed to keep most of the money.

In Switzerland, police discovered 100,000 Euros which had been shredded and were now blocking the toilets in Geneva. It had been flushed down by some Spanish citizens – talk about 'money laundering'!

HOW EXPLOSIVE IS THE FART?

Inspired by the Richter scale

1

Micro
Micro shaking which
is hardly felt

2

Minor
Felt slightly by some
people but no
damage

3

Minor
Shaking of indoor
objects can be
noticeable

4

Light
Rattling noises felt
by most people in
the affected area

5

Moderate
Can cause light
damage and is felt by
everyone

6

Strong
Violet shaking in the
epicentral area

7

Major
Felt across greater
distances with some
major damage

8

Great
Felt in extremely
large regions and
structures likely to
be destroyed

9

Extreme
Permanent changes
in ground
topography.
Thankfully only
occurs once every 10
years

SURPRISING!!

Almost all the giant pandas that exist in the world are owned by China. They rent about 50 of them out to other countries bringing in about a million dollars per year.

At the Humane Society of Missouri, kids volunteer to read books to nervous shelter dogs to make the dogs more likely to be adopted by families.

An avocado does not get ripe whilst it is still on the tree. They must be picked before they can ripen meaning that farmers can 'store' avocados on the tree itself.

Nikola Tesla, a pioneer in electricity and wireless information has a statue in Palo Alto, California that acts as a WiFi hotspot.

Cloaca Professional is an art and science exhibit that is fed real food and then replicates human digestion through a series of tubes and flasks. It has two 'stomachs' and defecates actual feces at the end.

Pizza

October is National Pizza Month

The volume of a pizza can be calculated with the formula of a cylinder $V=\pi r^2 h$, or with $V= Pi\ (z*z)\ a$, where Pi is 3.14, z for its radius, and a for its height. Hence, the word "pizza" is already the mnemonic for its volumetric formula.

In 2005, Italian Prime Minister Silvio Berlusconi insulted Finnish cuisine. In response, Kotipizza, a Finnish pizza restaurant chain, created a namesake pizza called "Pizza Berlusconi" which was topped with smoked reindeer, mushrooms, red onion, tomato sauce, and cheese. This pizza later won an International Pizza Contest.

The Japanese love to put mayonnaise on their pizza. It goes on the very top of the pizza in neat lines.

In India, the most popular pizza toppings are paneer (cottage cheese), mushrooms, peppers, onion, sweetcorn, pepperoni, sausage, black olives, extra cheese, and fresh garlic.

Fun Farty Facts

When Gerald Ford, 38th President of the United States, used to let one rip, he regularly blamed it on his Secret Service agents. He used to shout 'Was that you? Show some class!'

In the late 1800s, a Frenchman used to entertain his bakery customers with farts! He could actually make them sound like musical instruments. He even performed the act on stage.

How do you find out how much space a fart takes up? Scientists fed 10 volunteers with beans and then measured their flatulence over the next 24 hours. They decided farts measured 3 fluid ounces (90ml)

YOU FART ENOUGH IN A DAY TO FILL A BALLOON

Although, please don't gas up a fart balloon, please. On average, men fart around 12 times a day with a fart releasing anywhere from 30 milliliters to 200 milliliters of fart gas each.

The official name for fart gas is flatus which is made up of small amounts of hydrogen, carbon dioxide, and methane. It is, however, the ammonia that gives fart that smell. Ammonia is well known in chemistry to be a source of renewable fuel.

Yes. We can power machines with farts.

Also, it's impossible to hold in a fart. You can delay it for a while but as your guts gargle, in the end, the gas *will* escape. If you're lucky, it will go quietly and over a period of time so that no one suspects a thing. If you are unlucky, then the stinker you thought was under control will erupt in a loud uncontrollable fart.

You have been warned!

Yukky Things To Tell Your Friends

If Ancient Egyptians had toothache, they put a dead mouse in their mouth in an attempt to ease the pain

Albert Einstein's eyeballs are in a safety deposit box in New York City. They belong to Einstein's eye doctor and were removed at the autopsy

Castoreum is a substance secreted by beavers from a gland close to the anus. It is used in food as a substitute for vanilla, strawberry, and raspberry flavors.

In the UK, there is a law that pigeon poop belongs to the Crown. This is because it can be used to make gunpowder so King George I declared that the Crown would own all the excrement.

20% of US adults admit that they pee in swimming pools. Red eyes after swimming are a result of the pool chemicals mixing with the urine.

The original name of penicillin was 'mold juice'. It was found accidentally after Alexander Fleming left a petri dish and came back to discover a liquid around a mold had killed the bacteria

BIZARRE PEOPLE

In DC, there is an alternative universe where Bruce Wayne died instead of his parents.
This tragic incident implies that his father, Thomas Wayne, becomes Batman. His mother went so crazy after his death that she became the female version of The Joker.

On January 5, 2014, a Kentucky inmate named Robert Vick escaped prison and then turned himself in because it was too cold outside. It was only 3 degrees Fahrenheit(-16C) in Lexington that day with a fierce wind chill when he gave himself up at the Sunset Motel and Restaurant. The manager had to call the authorities twice before they believed his story.

A French entertainer named Michel Lotito (aka Mr. Eat-All) had an unusual eating disorder known as pica. It is a psychological disorder characterized by an appetite for substances that are largely indigestible. He had even eaten an entire Cessna 150 airplane although this took him 2 years. He ate bicycles, a shopping cart, chandeliers, a pair of skis, a bed, a brass plaque, a waterbed, a coffin with handles, and even a computer.

An American sideshow performer named Martin Joe Laurello could turn his head 120 degrees to the rear. He had the stage names of the Human Owl and Bobby the Boy with the Revolving Head.

Russian President Vladimir Putin has a black belt and is a taekwondo grandmaster however, he does not even practice the sport. The award is honorary and was bestowed on him during a visit to South Korea.

Zelma George of Canton, Ohio could write forward, backward, upside down, and upside down *and* backwards as well as any kind of different sentences in any direction using both her hands simultaneously.

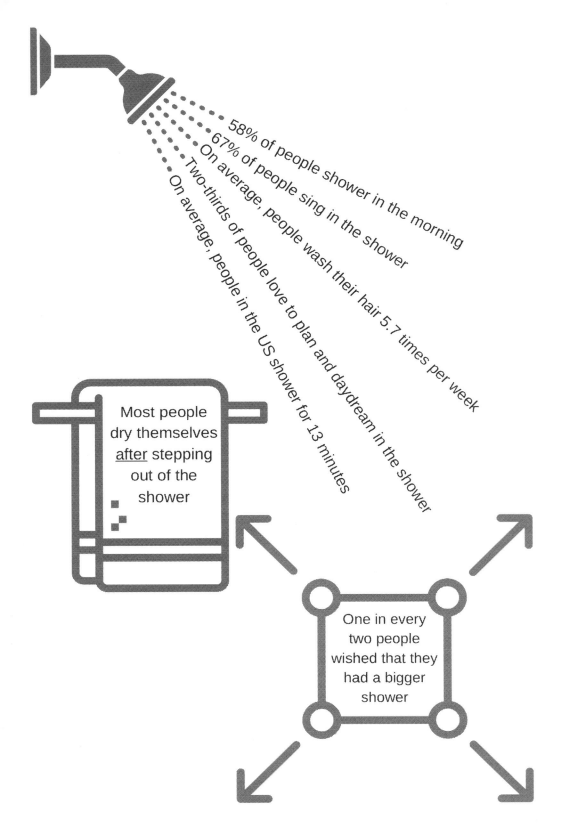

58% of people shower in the morning

67% of people sing in the shower

On average, people wash their hair 5.7 times per week

Two-thirds of people love to plan and daydream in the shower

On average, people in the US shower for 13 minutes

Most people dry themselves <u>after</u> stepping out of the shower

One in every two people wished that they had a bigger shower

MORE FACTS ABOUT MEDIEVAL BATHROOMS TO GROSS YOU OUT

CASTLE MOATS WERE JUST SEWERS Yep! Medieval castles were built so that any fancy toilets would discharge straight into the moat. Moats were kind of smelly but it put off invaders who had to cross the moat to get to the castle.

URINE WAS USED AS AN ANTISEPTIC. Medieval people even thought it would cure you from the plague. If you were wounded in battle, the doctor would come along and pee on your wounds! In actual fact, the ammonia in urine DID stop wounds from getting infected. An Italian soldier had his nose cut off in a fight and the doctor peed on it then sewed it back on and saved his nose. I wonder what he could smell?

NO-ONE WASHED HANDS BEFORE DINNER and on top of this, there were no forks and everyone used their hands to eat. How many times a day do you wash your hands?

THE MASTER OF THE CHAMBER was a high-ranking servant whose job it was to wipe the bottom of the King.

DOCTORS ORDERS - NO WASHING! Doctors told people that water made the body weak and the clean open pores of the skin allowed in disease including the black plague.

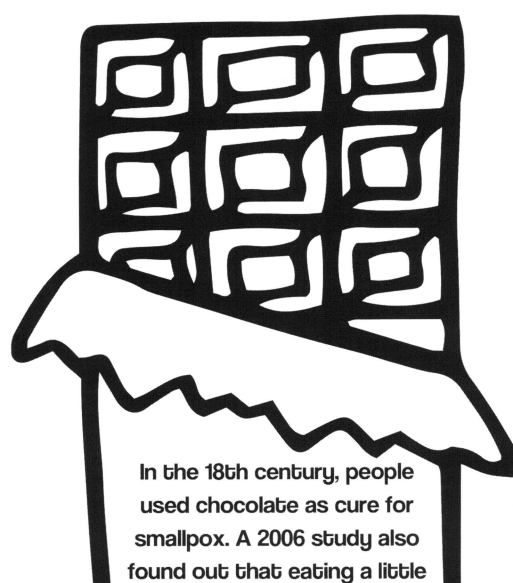

In the 18th century, people used chocolate as cure for smallpox. A 2006 study also found out that eating a little chocolate has a similar effect to taking an aspirin.

Other books by Alex Smart

Available on Amazon

www.thingstodowhileyoupoo.com

Other books by Alex Smart

Trivia book by Alex Smart for kids aged 8-88
Buy now on Amazon:
https://thingstodowhileyoupoo.com/

GET YOUR BONUS CONTENT

Enjoy 25 Pages of Bonus Content and sign up to get more goodies and freebies here:

https://thingstodowhileyoupoo.com/

About the author

Alex Smart has two adult 'kids' and lives in a small village in Devon, England with her patient husband.

She enjoys spending quality time with friends and family and likes to inject amusing games and quizzes into any social gathering.

Alex also enjoys making people smile with a gently mocking greeting card or novelty gift.

She created these books to be a fun and inexpensive gift for the 'hard to buy for' people in life.

"I love giving people fun gifts that make them laugh!"

3cd9a4d8-e440-49ec-9bf4-5e87a26c0c55R01

Made in the USA
Las Vegas, NV
19 December 2024